Night Walks

Helen Bednarz

BookLeaf Publishing

India | USA | UK

Presentation by *BookLeaf Publishing*

Web: www.bookleafpub.com

E-mail: info@bookleafpub.com

ISBN: 9789360948436

First edition 2024

To:

Mush,

Sparkle,

Jen,

and

Chimp.

Please take the world and make it yours.

ACKNOWLEDGEMENT

Thank you to Don Daiker for not only encouraging me to write, but to be a writer.

Thank you to the typewriters for so many nights of inspiration.

Thank you, dear friends, for calling my words poetry.

Thank you, Tess, for always being there for me.

PREFACE

Author image courtesy of Phillip Evans,
member of the

Pretentious Cleveland Portrait Artists

Cover image by Helen Bednarz

What is it Like?

It's like living in one of those forests from a
fairy tale
Darkness
Adventure
Magic
And much and much and much
The rustle of a long skirt.
Soft earth, the pine bark, snail slime sparking in
the trickles of sunlight that filter through the
trees.
Smells like sequoia and the cinnamon
mushroom smell of Thai jungles,

It's crowded and silent

I am a knight.
I am a thousand knights, each on a separate
quest.
I am the woman in the castle.
I have no hair to let down.
I am the strong and steady stones of the tower.

I ride.
We ride.
I watch them ride away.

And in this forest there is the gentle magic,
Sunlight and stream,
The distant smoke of a cottage hearth,
The rumble of hooves.

It's like being both sides of the army and the
wind.
And instead of war it becomes some strange
howling dance and feels
And feels
And feels like
No progress is made but we're all exhausted
And time, a giant hourglass, looms big as the
atmosphere above us all
Like the dual moons in a galaxy far away.

There is darkness and mystery,
Darting and skeptical eyes
The underside of a leaf

The hunter tracks a beast to slay it
Broken twigs,
The soft depression of a footprint on soil.

The beast weaves a flower wreath

I lie down on the bare ground and stare up at the
sky

Smile
Laugh at the nothing and everything
Smile
And deep sigh and when the beauty of it all hits
me the only thing to do is
chesttremble and cry
To be alive
To be alive on This Earth
To be alive

There is chatter

Of squirrel and bird. Sometimes there is so
much chatter. There is leaf roar and chainsaw
and talking and yelling and timber and
thunderstorm and a million radio stations and
sixteen novels speaking at the same time.
Sometimes there is a numb silence
And a thirsty tongue
Looking for words.

A hush falls.
One hand on piano keys
Plinks out a semi-familiar jazz melody.

Blinds clatter and raise
Windows of the sky open.
Another sunrise.

I want to tell you
I want to tell you
I want to tell…

I look around,
Bathed in light and glory,
Alone
Mostly
awash with the splendor of being alive.

I know it is temporary.
I kick at the edges of the sky,
Evaporate into spark and ash

Office Tome: Crickets

It is not the sound of nothing. It is hollow and
scraping.
       You can't see me but I am here.
You can never see them.
Sometimes the brown stains on the hem of your
dress from their spit.
Sometimes the nagging thoughts. You can't
sleep until you have answers.
Until there is silence on both sides of the
window.
There is not silence.
Not on either side.
Panes vibrate and pains vibrate
Chorus unsynchronized.
       We decide the song as we go.
There is no lulling, as the traffic quiets and lights
go out.
They seem to get louder. They begin to echo.
First in the ear canals. Then in the skill.
Then the jelly in your eye begins to wobble, not
in time with, but just behind
the trilling.
       But we are still searching
Sleep. You need sleep. These are supposed to
be the bright peaceful nights.

Before the summer ends.
And the screech, no, whistle. No, rattle. No,
song. No, call?
       I am still calling.
       I am tired, but I call.
       My legs ache and my antennae are
dewy.
You thought you liked this sound.
In books, it is romantic, or at least emblematic.
Now it just feels incessant.
And your eyes are burning from closing them so
hard to drown out the sound.
And the constriction in your chest gets too tired
to hold on.
       It is nice to meet you, too.
       Thank you, yes. I liked your song as
well.
       Sure, you can walk me home.
And from your warm body, your breath hums.
There is a slight rattle, or buzz. Or wheeze?
No, snore.

444

My dear child
It's 4:44
I could have never planned you
The confluence of post it notes, page markers,
sticky tack
[marking the idea behind each cell]
Each thing I ate as you grew in me
The race of my heart as I read at night, moved to
tears,
The stress of raised voices, the peace in the
smooth sunny trunk of my favorite tree.
So many factors shaping the expression of your
blueprint
A marvelous accident
A perfect plan
I never could have designed anything as
astonishing as you
My hands, bleeding ink of manifestations under
new moons,
even in their most wild and imaginative
moments,
could not have chosen you as precisely right as
you are.
And I could not have planned to love you as
much or as well or as intricately as I do.

No team of miners,
Minions from my brain,
could have excavated the space in my heart to fit
you as perfectly as what formed there naturally,
mineral deposits calcifying over lifetimes, to fit
you exactly
And then, oh miracle!
As you filled that space, how the edges soften,
the cave begins to breathe, and the space turns
out to be not underground but in the cosmos.

You're better than any chance happening I could
have dreamed.
In you I've confronted the limits of my vast
imagination and stand humbled and in awe at the
uncharted expanse before me

Love Story: Geographical

I've leaned on rivers
hoping they were mountains

January

The hourglass tips again.
I don't look forward to the falling of the grains.
I shake the table and
watch the glass tip over, one bulb --

crack and shatter and spill

moments across the table
like bone dust of a lifetime.
Peer closer and in each
there is minute discovery
in realization and moment
and there is sweetness:
in the smell of shucked peas
on my fingers,
the buckling of my knees on
the barefootfall on a sharp acorn.

On My Birthday

Wood nymph state of mind,
I am no goddess.
I don't want to be.

Spark and sparkle.

Rest. Sleep. Peace.

Time with my children, connecting in the wood
nymph state
True openness
Connection
Expansion
Opportunity to grow.

I sang in an airport bathroom stall

I won't stop my song.
I won't stop my heart
I won't stop my song.

We'll see the sunset and we're not supposed to
stop there.
We're supposed to step in.
It's there all the time.

You need to be listening.

No goddess imagery. What a gift to be mortal.
Imbuing each breath with a sacred scarcity that
creates capacity for abundance.
I am   all this power. Give me the grace that's
mud and bones
No celestial cheat codes

My body is the temple
What are we worshipping?
The limitedness
The impermanence
The capacity, the wonderful capacity.

TO BE INTERRUPTED BY CHILDREN.

Well, you know what they say…

"Dammit."

Map of the Building In Smells Today

1. Parking Space: Bus diesel
2. South Stairwell: Dust and sun
3. My Room: Palo Santo and espresso
4. Main Office: Vanilla, copy paper.
5. Front Courtyard: Hot metal and pollen
6. Upstairs Ladies' Restroom: Summer rain on a grassy field
7. First Floor Hallway: Dissection Week.
8. Peace Garden: Warm dirt, bees

Bug Lesson

Mud
daubers
stuff
paralyzed
spiders
into
the
nests
of their
young
to be
eaten.
Paralyzed
predators
to feed
the
children.

Now
THAT'S
Justice.

Love Languages

"Text me when you get home safe"
A follow up message after a nice evening, ping
before I even get home
"I can't wait to tell you…"
Warm water in my glass
Sees goosebumps; fetches blanket
Eggs
"Hurry! Come look at the sky!" (moon sunset
cloud)
The milk I like
Tucking me in anywhere– bed, couch, car
Touching my face, thumbs that caress
"Which face serum should I use?"
Looking over to see if I noticed
"I'm here to listen"
Tucking the blanket around my feet
"I really want to see you"
Coffee, mug handle first
"This smells like you"
Putting away the milk I left out
"Have you eaten? Make sure you eat."
Leaving a note or token for me to come home or
wake up to
"Will you teach me?"
A screenshot of the etymology of a fine word.

"I'm sorry, I know that was..."
Tucking my hair behind my ear
"I know a spot"
Asking for seconds
Asking questions

Love Languages, Also.

Love does not always win
Some love is squashed as it begins to grow
Some love is yeeted out of a third
or fourteenth story
or first floor window
Some love is ignored and left to languish.

Love is the spark of vision and possibility that
originates in each individual and extends
outward toward another.

Love does not always win.
Sometimes it runs away.

I Asked the Universe: "What would you like to tell me?"

What would you like to tell me?

We match our companions
They become our halos

I will dance.
I dance through all of life. I am a dancer. The
way I live my life is a dance.
       This is the music.
       It's all the music.

Everything in me was mine from the start.

And there's a graveyard of everything I no
longer am. But I carry a little pouch that
contains something of each corpse.
       A lock of hair.
       A tooth.
       A scrap of lace from the left sleeve.

And I don't need any more than those reminders.
     I am blessed to have my eyes,
       to no longer be exactly as I was,
       to have also been constant--
          As constant as the waves.

December 10th: "But What are Your Dreams?"

I'll tell you the truth: My dreams don't matter.

I don't need to have them.

My dreams are now. My dreams are every gift I currently have.

My dreams are alive in each breath and each choice.

My dreams are already realized
        Are just beginning
                Are constantly being rewritten.

I have choices whose muse I want to be
I have choices which dreams know my name

Love Story: Crepuscular Vows

From sunrises I enjoy alone
to sunsets we enjoy together
I promise to love you
with each solitary, fallen eyelash,
The crisp light of a planet on winter's night.
The swishes of my robe in my creeping
(you're still asleep).
I love you with the baseball bat I do not have.
I love you with words and song and windlasses.

Office Tome: Branch

River delta bleeds silver veins
        The glint of sunlight on white wings

Something like seeds inwind
neurons seeking and trembling on the stretch
toward each other.
        Lightning bridges across dendrites
Inwind.

Not upwind nor downwind but inwind.

Hair whipping into your eyes and feet lifting
All connections to gravity become questionable
because
now. Now you are inwind.

Inwind, you begine to unravel

the space between each sinew grows
Unnervingly.

On Your Next Birthday

Where did you find yourself?

Were you laughing at the sky?

Did you fall and tear your trousers?

Did anyone sing you a bouquet of old songs?

You are the first person to joyfully
invite me
to confront my strength.

Office Tome: Interjections

Interjections.
     (The arc of arms)
A graceful sweep-

A grape

Did we find the crepe paper for-

Can you make a heart on a typewriter?

Mostly they are questions.
     Or requests.
     Bid for a slice of time in the future
          (we are not promised)
     All the more urgent.

I used to read National Geographic with
ABSOLUTE
ZEAL.
(exclamation point)

And I positively still dream of a swim in a
cenote.

Have I told you about…?

But what I really mean by this interjection is

Here, trace with me the fingerprint of my life.

And what I mean by this question is
        Take my uncertainties and wonderings,
          Weave them like dark matter into
            night sky
                And we'll wonder at the stars
                we have made

How is there so much light, even at a new
moon?

And this thing I wish to share with you
    is to follow the lift of my eyelashes
    and see with me
    through them out into the wonders of the
world.

Anyway, grapes.

Coats

All my coats are dirty.

Coffee spills and dusty cuffs,
A smooch of ash across my
back from an industrial fire,
Mysterious brown smudges
down the thigh,
chest,
collar.
Cuffs are torn and dusty.

There's a twig in the faux fur trim.

Acorn caps in the pocket
of every coat
are not dirt
Nor the crumbles of pretty leaves
Nor the crushed sprigs of cypress
From another night walk.

Office Tome: Rabbits' Divorce

The glass had already shattered when I walked
in.

They sat on their haunches
Neither looked at me.
Neither looked at each other.

"Well?"

"WELL??"

I never noticed how long their eyelashes were.
But I did then. That quiet night.
Quiet except for the shattering glass.

whiskers quivered.

They signed the papers yesterday.

Winter Solstice

In the palm tree sway of longing,
Phantom warmth of sunlight echoes on my
cheeks,
I drift weightless in the blood-warm water at
daybreak.
Livingroom carpet.
Migraine constriction.
New breathtaking terrors
Bravery
Salt spray
Obliteration as simple as blowing ash
off a burned log
Never put back to tree again

Or maybe yes.

After years of transmutation

Fallout

An indistinct poison

It's time to wait
It's time to want small things only. Open to
explore.
Make connections.

I eat leaves and bridges.

Insidious nothingness

I'm here for my children. I'm here in the
credence
and ambiguities

Gathering strength
Collecting and concentrating power.
Whose eyes will be blinded
and whose opened?

Discovery

Feral Brain
Ferrari Brain

I dance. I'm language less,
Tongue flagging useless on the cobblestone
streets of Amsterdam,
Sanded raw on the brick roads of America.
Comfort and ease
A prison.
Locked knees.

I am.

Concussed and inflamed but there's more to
come and
(What if this works?)
The healing might be worth it.

I want to run a wall just to feel the confines of
my flesh,
Not self destructive, but informative.

This is the edge of a capillary. This is the skin
over the meat.
This is the wall.
This is the inkling.
This is the inside and the middle and the crush
of
Jawbone
And teeth and bitten lip and blood.

I am.

I see the child in you. I see the child in you, too.

It's endearing and sweet
(how strong is the man underneath?)

What child do you see in me?
Perpetual mother?
I lean in, I reject.
Maybe I am just the mother of men and children
and other people's children and plants and the
whole everything. Maybe I'm old as dirt and as
young as birth. Can I be both mother and child?

I am.

As fast and open as I am, I must hold my own
hand as I cross the street.

Lay your head in my lap in a restaurant.
(Come to think of it, I've never known another
person
To command the space in that way:
dim the lights, fix the table, throw the napkin,
dance with the soda fountain.
The way that I do.
That you do.
(We?)
It's thrilling and expansive and the way I like to
live.
But there will be no one to rein us in.
(Do I have reins?)
Are you a horse in want of a bridle?
Is anyone?)
Enkidu.
Enkidu

It is time to read the epic of Gilgamesh.

It is time to write more poetry by the light of day
and to speak smooth sauces and roux at night.
Speak the things I cannot eat.
Speak what I desires.
Speak what I wants you to paint.

It's past time to be afraid of it.

It is time for deserts and living things.
It is time, maybe, to drive pretty far and see
what happens.
It is time for citrus groves I've never smelled,
Red dirt sunrises.
It is time to go to the land of The Table Where
Rich People Sit.

And I am.

I want to know why we're so afraid of our
potential that we throw it away.
We measure and control,
Afraid of our power, our boundlessness.
Afraid of the changes it will bring.
There would be so many diamonds to insure.

We run against the walls to remind us of bounds
that don't exist.

You, ithink, can sense it too.

It is so fearsome to lose your mind.
To lose your mind to an accident.
A blink of an eye and a door, the blink of a knee
and a collapse.

There's terror in the aftermath that lingers.

Who am I now?
I'm not what I was.
I don't think like I did.
I long backwards for something that I don't even
know if I remember accurately.
I also love the me who is here now.
I bleed ink and disperse into the watercolor sky.

I am.

A big, stomping line. A series of questions

A ghost whispers:
Who are you anyway?
You're only who you decide to be.

Nothing is that isn't storytelling
and so, more than ever,
it is time to be the architect of those stories.
To stand with inky fingers and begin with

I am.